THE SOLOMON PORTFOLIO

HOW TO INVEST LIKE A KING

Published by DC Press
2445 River Tree Circle
Sanford, FL 32771
http://www.focusonethics.com

For orders other than individual consumers, DC Press grants discounts on purchases of 10 or more copies of single titles for bulk use, special markets, or premium use. For further details, contact:
Special Sales — DC Press
2445 River Tree Circle, Sanford, FL 32771
TEL: 866-602-1476

Cover Design: Jamie & Stephanie Katz
Composition by Jonathan Pennell
Book set in Adobe Trump Mediaeval

Library of Congress Catalog Number: 2008937100
Robert W. Katz
The Solomon Portfolio: How to Invest Like a King
ISBN: 978-1-932021-37-0

First DC Press Edition
10 9 8 7 6 5 4
Printed in the United States of America

THE SOLOMON PORTFOLIO

HOW TO INVEST LIKE A KING

BY

Robert W. Katz, CPA/PFS, MS

PRESS

A Division of the Diogenes Consortium

SANFORD • FLORIDA

DEDICATION

*This book is dedicated to my wife Jamie. If I were to look up in the dictionary the words **gift from God** your picture would be there. For over twenty-six years your love, support and respect has held me up and your faith has inspired me. I can never thank you too much or love you enough, but I will keep trying. I love you. Bob*

ACKNOWLEDGEMENTS

This book could not have been written without the brilliant work of Professor Craig Israelsen of Brigham Young University. His insightful work has raised the work that I do to a new level. However, it has been his willingness to freely share his reserach that has revealed his outstanding character and integrity. I am honored by our new frienship.

And, no book that I have written would be complete without acknowledging three pastors who have so willingly poured their lives into mine. Pastor Charles Green, Pastor Mike Mille' and Pastor Steve Robinson. I can never thank you enough for your support, mentoring, love, correction, and wisdom.

CONTENTS

Dedication...v

Acknowledgements...vii

Foreword by Pat Roberson xi

Introduction – The Solomon Portfolio...................................xv

1. The More Things Change the More they Remain the Same......1

2. The Missing Piece...11

3. Building Blocks 17

4. Asset Class One: Large Capitalization U.S. Stocks...................25

5. Asset Class Two: Small Capitalization U.S. Stocks 37

6. Asset Class Three: Non-U.S. Stocks 41

7. Asset Class Four: Commodities......................................45

8. Asset Class Five: Real Estate 49

9. Asset Class Six: Cash 53

10. Asset Class Seven: Intermediate Bonds............................59

11. The Solomon Portfolio 65

12. The Eighth Portion — Reader's Gift...............................69

Epilogue..73

Contact Information..75

About the Author 77

FOREWORD

Bob has been a personal friend and friend of CBN for many years. He has also been a guest on *The 700 Club* discussing Bible based financial planning and stewardship. Among his prior books has been the best seller, *Money Came by the House the Other Day*, which has touched the lives of thousands of Christians by teaching them vital scriptural financial principles to guide them through the various financial seasons of their lives.

It is a pleasure to write the introduction for Bob's newest book, *The Solomon Principle, How to Invest Like a King*. This book takes the wisdom of the richest and wisest man that ever lived, King Solomon, and couples it with amazing modern day research which proves that Solomon's investment principles are still today the best investment advice available.

The Solomon Portfolio may be the only book on investing you will ever need. It is easy to understand, easy to apply, and appropriate for almost any investment scenario. *The Solomon Portfolio* takes the mystery out of investing and teaches you now to invest your assets with the optimal combination of high return and low risk.

—Pat Roberson
CBN, Chairman of the Board

"King Solomon was greater in riches and wisdom than all the other kings of the earth. The whole world sought audience with Solomon to hear the wisdom God had put in his heart."

—1 Kings 10:23-24

INTRODUCTION

I RECENTLY READ A STORY about a young man who greatly admired Warren Buffet. He had studied all of Mr. Buffet's writings, went to his annual meetings in Omaha and even had pictures of Mr. Buffet hanging on the wall in his office. Nothing wrong with that, Mr. Buffet is a financial genius. I have heard similar stories regarding people who admire Bill Gates, Steven Job, Donald Trump, and so many more of our American financial heroes.

In terms of wanting to be financially successful there is nothing wrong with studying those who have already attained financial success. I have long believed that if you want to learn how to do something with excellence, find someone who is already a success and doing it with excellence, and study what they do. Then apply it to your own life.

But, here is another interesting story.

"That night God appeared to Solomon and said to him, "Ask for whatever you want me to give you." Solomon answered God, "you have shown great kindness to David my father and have made me king in his place. Now, Lord God, let your promise to my father David be confirmed, for you have made me king over a people who are as numerous as the dust of the earth. Give me wisdom and knowledge, that I may lead this people, for who is able to govern this great people of yours?" God said to Solomon, "Since this is your heart's desire and

you have not asked for wealth, riches or honor, nor for the death of your enemies, and since you have not asked for a long life but for wisdom and knowledge to govern my people over whom I have made you king, **therefore wisdom and knowledge will be given to you. And I will also give you wealth, riches and honor, such as no king who was before you ever had and none after you will have.***"*

—2 Chronicles 1:7-12 (emphasis added)

In this true story King David has passed away and the mantle of kingship falls upon his young son Solomon. Solomon is overwhelmed by the enormity of the task of ruling over Israel at such a young age. God, in His mercy appears to Solomon in a dream and instructs him to ask for whatever he wants and the Lord will give it to him. Of all the things that Solomon could have asked for he asks for wisdom and knowledge. The Lord is so pleased by his unselfish request that He grants the request, and then says I will also give you what you did not ask for namely, riches and honor unlike anyone has ever had or will ever have.

I submit to you that in three or four hundred years very few people, if any, will know who Warren Buffet was. Yet, three thousand years later the world still knows that the richest and wisest man to ever live was King Solomon.

Solomon was wise enough to know that his wisdom and riches came from understanding and applying the eternal principles that the Lord revealed to him through His Word. We should be that wise as well.

This book, using a very easy to understand and practical approach, will take the investment principles that the Lord revealed to King Solomon and teach you how to apply them to your own investments.

These principles are instructions straight from the Word of God. Three thousand years later they are still there to teach you how to construct your own Solomon Portfolio and How *To Invest Like a King*.

CHAPTER

1

THE MORE THINGS CHANGE THE MORE THEY REMAIN THE SAME

"What has been will be again, what has been done will be done again; there is nothing new under the sun".

—Ecclesiastes 1:9

It never fails to amaze me.

I have been a practicing CPA for over thirty years. During that time I have counseled with thousands of people on virtually every aspect of financial planning and stewardship. In all of that time I have never once been asked a question about finances or stewardship where the answer could not be found in the Bible.

Five thousand years of God's infallible Word is there just waiting for us to apply it to our lives. Yet, all too often we chase after the latest hot stock tip or the advice of the most currently popular financial author or television personality. We unquestionably follow the advice of a stockbroker, financial advisor, banker, insurance agent or Uncle Charlie while we push God's Word to the side writing it off as not applicable, out dated and archaic.

Yet, nothing could be further from the truth. There are over twenty-five hundred references to finances and stewardship in the Bible and over half of the parables deal with financial issues. And, Biblical advice is timeless. God tells us in **Malachi 3:6**, *"I the Lord do not change."* His Word is the same yesterday, today and forever. So I ask you from what better source is there to receive financial advice than the perfect Word of God?

There is none.

Almost daily I am involved with helping people invest their funds. It is a responsibility that I take very seriously. Therefore, investing is a topic that I constantly study and pray about.

Even if you are not a "religious" person, but have read to this point, I urge you to read further.

As I stated in the introduction to this book, I have always believed that if you want to do something with excellence, find someone who is already doing it with excellence and study what they do. When it comes to investing certainly the starting place should be to study King Solomon. *What better role model to teach us about investing than the richest and wisest man that ever lived?* There is probably more financial wisdom in the books of Ecclesiastes and Proverbs than in most of the financial books that have ever been written combined.

The truth is the secret to successful investing begins over three thousand years ago at **Ecclesiastes 11:1-2** with King Solomon telling us:

"Cast your bread upon the waters, for after many days you will find it again. Give portions to seven, yes to eight, for you do not know what disaster may come upon the land."

Simply put, Solomon is telling us to diversify. Thousands of years later we now call it *asset allocation*, but the principle is unchanging, don't put all of your eggs in one basket. This is also the first written record of the investment principle of correlation, something we will discuss in the next chapter.

I have always believed in asset allocation or proper diversification of your investments. Modern day studies have confirmed that up to ninety-four percent of the gain on your investments comes from the proper allocation of your assets.

The truth is, no matter what you are told to the contrary, no one is smart enough to consistently outperform the financial market. No one, no system, no software is going to be able to accurately tell you what to invest in, when to buy it and when to sell it. The key to proper investing is to properly diversify into many different types of investments and then to sit back and prudently monitor your investments. This is commonly referred to as a "buy and hold" strategy. Selling of your investments should only take place when there is a financial need for funds, or if there is a substantial change for the worse in one of your investments.

If you believe in asset allocation the question then becomes, "How do I properly allocate my assets?" In other words what are the various types of investments that I should use to diversify my portfolio?

I have prayed about and studied this scripture for years longing to have asked questions such as, "Solomon, what are the core seven asset classes you are referring to" And, why did you add the phrase "yes eight"?

I have always had a general idea about what the seven asset classes were, but I continued to search for certainty. As I continued to research, study and pray for confirmation regarding *the specific* seven core asset classes that everyone should be invested in, it happened.

As I was studying one day I came across a brilliant article written by Craig Israelsen, a professor at Brigham Young University. Dr. Israelsen had decided to study various asset allocations, such as a one asset portfolio (all cash), two asset portfolio (cash and bonds), three asset portfolio (cash, bonds and large U.S. stocks) etc., up to a seven asset class portfolio. He also studied traditional portfolio mixes such as 60% stocks and 40% bonds and 40% stocks and 60% bonds. He studied a total of ten possible portfolio combinations and then back tested each portfolio for 38 years. That is, he compiled statistical data on each portfolio for the last 38 years in order to determine which portfolio would have produced the highest return on your investments with the lowest amount of risk (See Illustration 1). His work is also broken down on a year by year basis for the last 38 years at Illustration 2.

Now, here is the truly amazing conclusion to his study that was like an arrow of revelation piercing me as I read his study.

OVER THE LAST 38 YEARS WHEN YOU LOOK AT YIELD AND RISK TOGETHER, THE ABSOLUTE BEST PORTFOLIO ALLOCATION PROVIDING AN AVERAGE YIELD OF 11.16% AND A STANDARD DEVIATION FOR RISK OF ONLY 8.6 WAS *THE SEVEN ASSET PORTFOLIO.*

Think about it. Unknowingly, Dr. Israelsen's research has served to travel back over 3,000 years of recorded history to confirm what scripture has already told us, *"Give portions to seven"*. God's Word is truth and ultimate wisdom, and it never changes.

The Lord gave this information to Solomon. Solomon wrote it down as instructions for all future generations. And, I believe that the

Lord has used Dr. Israelsen to confirm Solomon's advice using "scientific research" for a world that needs "hard facts".

Here are the seven specific asset types that produce this amazing result, which I call:

THE SOLOMON PORTFOLIO

1) Large-cap U.S. stocks
2) Small-cap U.S. stocks
3) Non-U.S. stocks
4) Commodities and Natural Resources
5) Real Estate Investment Trusts (REITs)
6) Intermediate bonds
7) Cash

For purposes of this book all seven investment classes should be invested and maintained in equal portions. Dr. Israelsen is working on a book where he will use the same seven core asset classes in different percentages to create four new portfolios: very conservative, conservative, moderate and aggressive. The book will be entitled the *7/Twelve, A Portfolio for Life* and I highly recommend that you purchase it when published.

The Solomon Portfolio is simple. This straightforward scriptural advice is the most appropriate way to invest for almost all of your financial goals such as retirement, saving for your children's education costs, investing most trust assets or just for investing your long-term personal savings.

The purpose of this book is twofold. First, it is to teach you about each of the asset classes that comprise The Solomon Portfolio. Second, it will teach you how to construct The Solomon Portfolio in an easy, straightforward and cost effective manner using no-load mutual funds, exchange traded funds (ETFs) and exchange traded notes (ETNs).

Equally-Weighted Assets in Retirement Withdrawal Portfolio ($500,000 starting balance, 5% withdraw rate, 3% inflation rate of annual withdrawal)	38-Year IRR (%) 1970-2007	38-Year Standard Deviation of Annual Returns (%)	
One-Asset Portfolio 100% Cash	7.04	3.08	
Equal-Weighted Two-Asset Portfolio 50% each: Cash & Bonds	7.71	3.63	
Equal-Weighted Three-Asset Portfolio 33% each: Cash, Bonds, Large US Stock	8.69	6.44	
Equal-Weighted Four-Asset Portfolio 25% each: Cash, Bonds, Large US Stock, Small US Stock	9.49	9.33	
Equal-Weighted Five-Asset Portfolio 20% each: Cash, Bonds, Lrg US, Sml US, Non-US Stock	9.89	10.34	
Equal-Weighted Six-Asset Portfolio 16.7% each: Cash, Bonds, Lrg US, Sml US, Non-US, REIT	10.24	10.58	
Equal-Weighted Seven-Asset Portfolio (EW) 14.3% each: Cash, Bonds, Lrg US, Sml US, Non-US, REIT, Commodities	11.16	8.60	
Custom-Weighted Seven-Asset Portfolio (CW) 20% Cash, 40% Bonds, 12% Lrg US, 8% Sml US, 10% Non-US, 5% REIT, 5% Commodities	9.64	5.92	
Conservative 40/60 Allocation 40% Large US Stock, 60% Bond	9.32	8.02	
Moderate 60/40 Allocation 60% Large US Stock, 40% Bond	9.66	10.66	

[a]Worst case single year portfolio draw-down is a measure of the percentage change in the ending portfolio value from the end of one year to the end of the next year after considering the annual withdrawal. This measure is dependent on the prior year. **Illustration 1 Developed by Craig Israelsen Ph.D.**

Aggregate Portfolio Correlation	Worst-Case One-Year Portfolio Drawdown (%)[a] (Year Worst Loss Occurred)	Frequency of Loss (Percentage of years portfolio lost value as measured by % change in year end-to-year end account balance)	Average Annual % Loss
—	(13.9) (2007)	53%	(4.4)
0.41	(3.4) (2004)	24%	(2.0)
0.22	(9.4) (1974)	18%	(4.3)
0.25	(14.2) (1974)	24%	(5.3)
0.23	(16.9) (1974)	21%	(8.0)
0.26	(18.8) (1974)	16%	(10.0)
0.13	(10.2) (1974)	21%	(3.9)
0.13	(7.3) (1974)	16%	(2.6)
0.22	(12.2) (1974)	21%	(4.7)
0.22	(18.8) (1974)	26%	(6.6)

Table 5. Portfolio Progression in a Retirement Distribution Portfolio (1970-2007) (*In those years with a loss in account value*)

Year	Large US Equity	Small US Equity	Non-US Equity	Intermediate Term US Bonds	
1970	3.92	(17.40)	(11.66)	16.90	
1971	14.14	16.50	29.59	8.70	
1972	19.16	4.40	36.35	5.20	
1973	(14.69)	(30.90)	(14.92)	4.60	
1974	(26.47)	(19.90)	(23.16)	5.70	
1975	37.23	52.80	35.39	7.80	
1976	23.64	57.40	2.54	12.90	
1977	(7.44)	25.40	18.06	3.00	
1978	6.40	23.50	32.62	2.23	
1979	18.30	43.07	4.75	6.59	
1980	32.22	38.60	22.58	6.65	
1981	(5.08)	2.03	(2.28)	10.79	
1982	21.46	24.95	(1.86)	25.42	
1983	22.46	29.13	23.69	8.22	
1984	6.26	(7.30)	7.38	14.29	
1985	31.74	31.05	56.16	18.00	
1986	18.68	5.68	69.44	13.06	
1987	5.26	(8.80)	24.63	3.61	
1988	16.61	25.02	28.27	6.40	
1989	31.68	16.26	10.54	12.68	
1990	(3.12)	(19.48)	(23.45)	9.56	
1991	30.48	46.04	12.13	14.11	
1992	7.62	18.41	(12.17)	6.93	
1993	10.06	18.88	32.56	8.17	
1994	1.31	(1.82)	7.78	(1.75)	
1995	37.53	28.45	11.21	14.41	
1996	22.94	16.49	6.05	4.06	
1997	33.35	22.36	1.78	7.72	
1998	28.57	(2.55)	19.93	8.49	
1999	21.04	21.26	27.03	0.49	
2000	(9.10)	(3.02)	(14.19)	10.47	
2001	(11.88)	2.49	(21.42)	8.42	
2002	(22.09)	(20.48)	(15.94)	9.64	
2003	28.67	47.25	38.59	2.29	
2004	10.71	18.33	20.25	2.33	
2005	4.91	4.55	13.54	1.68	
2006	15.79	18.37	26.34	3.84	
2007	5.49	(1.60)	11.20	8.47	
38-Year Average Annualized % Return	11.03	11.74	10.86	8.08	
38-Year Standard Deviation of Annual Returns	16.61	21.69	21.54	5.43	
Number of Years with a Negative Return	8	11	10	1	
Worst One-Year % Return	(26.47)	(30.90)	(23.45)	(1.75)	
Worst Three-Year Cumulative % Return	(37.59)	(42.22)	(43.32)	6.43	

Illustration 2. Developed by Craig Israelsen Ph.D.

	Cash	REIT	Commodities	All 7 Assets in Equal-Weighted Portfolio
	6.80	(4.00)	15.17	1.39
	4.52	15.52	20.15	15.59
	4.23	8.01	42.37	17.10
	7.46	(15.52)	74.90	1.56
	8.35	(21.42)	39.50	(5.34)
	6.08	19.29	(17.22)	20.20
	5.23	47.56	(11.94)	19.62
	5.52	22.43	10.38	11.05
	7.67	10.34	31.56	16.33
	10.86	35.86	33.78	21.89
	12.71	24.36	11.06	21.17
	15.58	6.02	(22.98)	0.58
	11.66	21.60	11.57	16.40
	9.24	30.64	16.23	19.94
	10.33	20.93	1.03	7.56
	7.97	19.07	10.02	24.86
	6.29	19.17	2.05	19.20
	6.13	(3.65)	23.76	7.28
	7.06	13.47	27.92	17.82
	8.67	8.84	38.25	18.13
	7.99	(15.34)	29.13	(2.10)
	5.68	35.69	(6.13)	19.71
	3.59	14.58	4.41	6.20
	3.12	19.67	(12.32)	11.45
	4.45	3.17	5.28	2.63
	5.79	15.25	20.32	18.99
	5.26	35.26	33.90	17.71
	5.31	20.28	(14.09)	10.96
	5.01	(17.51)	(35.71)	0.89
	4.87	(4.62)	40.89	15.85
	6.32	26.36	49.71	9.51
	3.67	13.93	(31.91)	(5.24)
	1.68	3.81	32.03	(1.62)
	1.05	37.14	20.68	25.10
	1.43	31.59	17.28	14.56
	3.34	12.17	25.69	9.41
	4.80	35.06	(15.09)	12.73
	4.33	(15.69)	32.67	6.41
	6.27	12.60	11.99	11.39
	3.08	17.16	23.91	8.60
	0	8	9	4
	1.05	(21.42)	(35.71)	(5.34)
	4.22	(28.30)	(26.04)	2.09

CHAPTER

2

THE MISSING PIECE

"There is a time for everything, and a season for every activity under heaven."

—Ecclesiastes 3:1

I see it all too often.

A couple comes into my office for financial counseling and asks me to look at their current investment portfolio. Usually, what I see is a portfolio constructed of stocks, mutual funds and bonds. After all what else is there to consider in an investment portfolio? Even good financial advisors with good intentions tend to take a very standardized approach to constructing an investment portfolio.

The first step for a financial advisor should be to get to know your client's needs and wants. This is usually accomplished through a series of meetings and by walking the client through financial questionnaires. There is nothing wrong with this because it is vital that an advisor understand the true financial needs and goals of their client **and their client's tolerance for risk**. Two clients may be in very similar financial situations, however, if their tolerance for risk is significantly different, often it will need to be reflected in their investment portfolio.

After an advisor has assessed a client's needs and risk tolerance the next step is to agree on a basic asset allocation. That allocation has historically been made between equities (in the form of stocks or mutual funds) and fixed income investments (usually in the form of cash, various types of bonds and/or certificates of deposit). You will often hear investment portfolios described in terms of their asset allocation. For instance, a standard conservative portfolio may be referred to as a 40/60 allocation, that is, 40% invested in equities and 60% invested in fixed income investments. Likewise, a moderate allocation portfolio is often referred to as a 60/40 portfolio. It is invested 60% in equities and 40% in fixed income investments. Aggressive portfolios are usually 80% in equities / 20% in fixed income investments.

This approach is standard throughout the investment industry **AND HEREIN LIES THE FUNDAMENTAL FLAW THAT SOLOMON WARNED US ABOUT THOUSANDS OF YEARS AGO:**

> *"....for you do not know what disaster may come upon the land.'*

—Ecclesiastes 11:2b

Solomon, in his wisdom, was the first person to ever write about a crucial investment concept that we now call **CORRELATION**. When portfolios are constructed solely on the basis of how much money should be invested in equities and how much in fixed income investments a vital piece of the allocation process is missing. The technical term for that missing piece, as I have said, is called *correlation*.

Correlation is really a simple concept. It refers to a statistical measurement of how likely the investments in your portfolio are to move in the same direction as markets go up and down. The closer the correlation is to "0" (on a scale that ranges from -1 to 1) the more likely investments are to move in the same direction. As correlations approach "0" your investments tend not to be tied together and will move in different directions which significantly reduces risk.

Here is an example of how correlation works. Most of the time when a client brings a portfolio to me from another investment advisor, the asset allocation is acceptable. For discussion purposes let's say it is a typical 60/40 moderate allocation portfolio. All appears well so far. But, as I look at what comprises the "60%" in equities I almost always find that the advisor has invested the funds in some large-cap stocks, mid-cap stocks, small-cap stocks, and international stocks and therefore concludes that he has constructed a diversified portfolio. Not true. When we start to look at the correlation between those various types of equities we find that they are highly correlated. That is, if the market is going up, these investments will all increase in value at the same time. However, if the market is moving down, they will all lose value together. While you may think your portfolio is diversified, the truth is, it is not, because 60% of it or more is so highly correlated. See Illustration 3 for correlations between the seven core asset classes of The Solomon Portfolio.

Harry Markowitz, who is famous for his modern day portfolio allocation work simply puts it ,"To reduce risk, it is necessary to avoid a portfolio whose securities are all highly correlated with each other." (Markowitz, 1991, *Portfolio Selection*, Blackwell Publishing).

Ideally, as we construct a portfolio, our goal is to achieve the lowest overall correlation possible. That is, if some of our investments are going down in value, others should be going up.

This brings us back to King Solomon. When the Lord spoke to Solomon and told him to allocate his holdings into "portions of seven," He knew that this would produce the optimal lowest correlation. Fast forward 3,000 years and look at Illustration 1 again and you will see that the seven asset class Solomon Portfolio does indeed have the lowest correlation score, a mere .13.

The importance of correlation is even more clearly demostrated when we look at Illustration 2 once again. Here Dr. Israelsen takes each of the seven asset classes and shows us how they performed during each of the 38 years he studied. What we see is correlation plainly evident. Notice that in almost every year where one asset class does poorly, another asset class will do well. For instance, let's look at 1974, one of the worst years for investing in the last forty years. If you had just invested in stocks you would have lost a considerable amount of money (somewhere between 19.9% and 26.47% of your funds). However, if you had followed King Solomon's advice and invested in a seven asset class portfolio, even during this terrible year, you would have only lost 5.34%. Notice that in all thirty eight years studied in Illustration 2 the worst year of all sustained only a 5.34% loss. **Correlation** is the key...the wisdom is the Lord's.

The next seven chapters are going to teach you to construct a cost efficient seven asset class portfolio using highly rated no-load mutual funds and exchange traded funds and notes (ETFs & ETNs). Each chapter will discuss a separate asset class. The chapter will end with examples of assets that represent that class. It is IMPORTANT to note that the examples are exactly that, EXAMPLES. Do not use these examples just because they appear in this book. As time passes some funds will lose their high ranking and others will gain it. You must do your own homework on selecting individual investments for each asset class. This book will help you to learn how to do that, but the responsibility for ultimate selection is still yours. The Lord has placed you as steward over certain assets He has entrusted into your care and you are never to totally delegate that authority to anyone else. The purpose of this book is to provide wise counsel in order to prepare you to be the ultimate decision maker.

Before I ever make any investment I follow this scriptural process based on the warning of the prophet Hosea,

"...my people are destroyed from lack of knowledge."

—Hosea 4:6

1. I study the investment to show myself approved.

"Study and be eager and do your utmost to present yourself to God approved (tested by trial), a workman who has no cause to be ashamed, correctly analyzing and accurately dividing rightly handling and skillfully teaching the Word of Truth."|

—2 Timothy 2:15 (Amplified)

2. I pray for wisdom, guidance and confirmation from the Holy Spirit

"But when he, the Spirit of truth, comes, he will guide you into all truth."

—John 16:13

3. I pray with my wife to make sure we are in agreement.

"Do two walk together unless they have agreed to do so?"

—Amos 3:3

Subsequently, I only invest after these three scriptural principles form a foundation for the investment decisions I am about to make. I urge you to do the same.

38-Year Correlations (Using Annual Returns from 1970-2007)

	Large US Equity	Small US Equity	Non-US Equity	US Bonds	Cash	REIT
Small US Equity	0.739					
Non-US Equity	0.586	0.470				
US Bonds	0.220	0.063	-0.100			
Cash	0.046	0.014	-0.122	0.407		
REIT	0.462	0.757	0.297	0.104	-0.050	
Commodities	-0.281	-0.318	-0.145	-0.210	-0.001	-0.271

Aggregate Portfolio Correlation Among all Seven Assets = 0.13

Illustration 3 Developed by Craig Israelsen, Ph.D.

CHAPTER

3

BUILDING BLOCKS

"Study and be eager and do your utmost to present yourself to God approved (tested by trial), a workman who has no cause to be ashamed, correctly analyzing and accurately dividing—rightly handling and skillfully teaching—the Word of Truth."

—2 Timothy 2:15

Before we begin to discuss the specific investments that make up the seven asset classes of the Solomon Portfolio we need to have an understanding of some basic concepts. Each of the seven asset classes will be represented by no-load mutual funds, exchange traded funds and exchange traded notes, and fixed income investments. Therefore, a general word of explanation about each is necessary.

This book assumes that the reader has a general understanding of what stocks, bonds, mutual funds and exchange traded funds and exchange traded notes are. It is not intended to be a course on each of these types of investments. If you do not have a strong understanding of these investments or just want to learn more, I suggest that you read some of the excellent books on these types of investments such as:

Morningstar Guide to Mutual Funds, Benz, Di Teresa, and Kinnel, 2003

Mutual Funds for Dummies, Eric Tyson, 2007

Common Sense on Mutual Funds, John C. Bogle, 1999

There are, of course, many more, but these will do a fine job in getting you started on understanding exactly what each of the seven core asset classes represents.

★ ★ ★ ★

Stock markets (equities) are a fundamentally sound concept. They allow corporations to efficiently raise capital and individuals to share in the economic success of the corporations they believe in. It is this easy access to corporate capital coupled with individual investment opportunity that has set the stage for the United States to be the most economically successful nation in the history of the world. Many other nations are now seeing that free markets are the most efficient means to raise the standard of living for their citizens. Stock markets are a fundamentally good idea.

But, something has happened over the last forty years. For many people the stock market has become America's great casino, where the notion of investing has been pushed aside and replaced by the urge to make a "quick killing" in the market. Just as the Las Vegas gaudy neon lights lure gamblers, tails of **how** to make a fortune in the stock market seduce the unwary investor.

Almost daily, corporations with little experience and weak business plans place their newly issued stock into the market for sale. And, everyday, billions of dollars are invested by investors with little or no concept of what a stock is or whether the purchase they are making is suitable for their needs. And so, we have a fundamentally sound concept being manipulated and pushed to extremes by greed and lack of knowledge. When any market reaches an extreme, there will always be a subsequent adjustment or collapse.

Am I telling you not to buy stocks? Not at all. In fact, most of the *Solomon Portfolio* will be comprised of high quality stock and "stock like" investments. The stock market has historically provided a better return on investment than any other class of asset. However, before you buy a single share of stock you must thoroughly understand what you are investing in and how you are going to invest in it.

The great prophet Hosea warned us and it bears repeating over and over again:

"...my people are destroyed from lack of knowledge."

—Hosea 4:6

And, **Proverbs 3:13-17** promises us,

"Blessed is the man who finds wisdom, the man who gains understanding, for she is more profitable than silver and yields better returns than gold. She is more precious than rubies; nothing you desire can compare with her. Long life is in her right hand; and in her left hand are riches and honor. Her ways are pleasant ways and all her paths are peace."

The purpose of this chapter is to provide you with a basic overview of stocks and fixed income investments and to instruct you on how to best invest in them.

STOCKS

Someone has a good idea. Sam Walton (the founder of Wal-Mart) thinks people might like stores that offer virtually everything at "everyday low prices". Bill Gates (the co-founder of Microsoft) thinks his software operating system is the best in the world. Starbucks thinks that people would like to sit around and leisurely drink gourmet coffee. All are great concepts, but to bring the concept to reality, the visionary founders of these companies all shared a common need. They needed money and lots of it. In order to raise that money they decided to offer shares of their corporations to the general public.

Stocks are nothing more than a fractional ownership interest in a company. The more shares you own, the more of the company you own.

The vast majority of stocks are referred to as *Common Stocks*. Common stock represents a general ownership in a corporation and usually provides the shareholder with no preferential rights. Common shareholders share in the general success or failure of the companies in which they have invested. If a company is successful, the shareholder's financial reward for the risk they have assumed may come in two forms. A shareholder may receive a dividend (cash payment from the corporation) based on the number of shares they own. A shareholder may also share in the growth of the value of those shares. This increase in the value of a stock is generally referred to as a capital gain or capital appreciation.

Common stocks are further defined by dividing them into several categories and sub-categories. Categories may be based on the size of the underlying company such as large and small-cap stocks. Another common category deals with the "investment objective" of a stock, such as, a *growth* or *value* stock. We will deal with these categories in much more detail in the next seven chapters.

Having said all of this, the question at hand is, "Are individual stocks right for you?"

The answer is that individual stocks are not suitable for most investors.

Although the stock market has outperformed virtually every other asset class over the last 100 years, the truth is that most individual investors lose money in the stock market because they are *playing the market and not investing in it.*

Most individual investors do not have the time, knowledge and/or mental discipline to trade individual stocks. That is why I strongly urge the majority of investors to construct their Solomon Portfolio with *no-load mutual funds* and *exchange traded funds and notes* (ETFs and ETNs).

MUTUAL FUNDS

Somewhere, some time ago, someone got a bright idea concerning risk sharing and diversification. Prior to this bright idea if you had $5,000 to invest you'd probably be limited to purchasing one or two stocks. However, if you pooled your money with hundreds of other investors, that pool of funds could now purchase a varied portfolio of stocks and spread the risk of loss accordingly—thus the birth of the mutual fund industry.

The primary advantage of mutual funds is that they are managed by professional advisors. This relieves the individual investor from having to comb through research on thousands of individual stocks. However, it is still the responsibility of the investor to research the mutual funds they are considering investing in. The good news is that this is a much easier process than individual stock analysis.

Virtually every business magazine will have an issue dealing with mutual funds. In it they almost always analyze funds according to various criteria and recommend those funds that they believe will perform the best in years to come. This is often a good place to begin your research.

However, without a doubt, Morningstar, Inc,. a Chicago based investment research firm, is known for its in-depth, ongoing, and objective research and analysis of mutual funds. If you know very little about investing in mutual funds I highly recommend that you read their book, *Morningstar Guide to Mutual Funds*. Their website **www.morningstar.com** provides a wealth of information on mutual funds and offers subscriptions to their various excellent research services.

EXCHANGE TRADED FUNDS AND NOTES

Another potentially excellent investment vehicle for your Solomon Portfolio is Exchange Traded Funds and Notes (ETFs and ETNs). An ETF is very similar to a mutual fund in that it represents a basket of stocks. Unlike mutual funds which are sold at their net asset value at the end of each day, ETFs can be bought and sold anytime during the trading day at their then current price. In this regard an ETF trades like a stock. Since it trades like a stock you typically recognize little or no capital gains distributions for tax purposes at the end of each year like you would with a mutual fund. ETFs are passively managed index securities that trade on stock exchanges. That is, the fund is constructed to reflect an index or basket of stocks, such as the S&P 500, and little or no trading is done within the fund once established. There are now literally hundreds of ETFs which reflect a myriad of indexes such as large-cap stocks, small-cap stocks, international stocks, energy stocks, technology stocks, etc. Since they are passively managed, the management fees are generally very inexpensive.

A disadvantage of ETFs is that you pay a commission every time you buy and sell them, so you have to be aware of the additional trading costs involved. However, to me the primary disadvantage of an ETF, is that right now, they are constructed to reflect indexes such as the S&P 500. Since ETFs reflect averages, you can almost always find a "Morningstar," five star rated," no-load mutual fund that will out-perform a comparable ETF. I use ETFs primarily in cases where there are no no-load funds that accomplish the investment objectives I am seeking to fill, such as in the area of commodities. Again, we will go into this in greater detail in the next seven chapters.

Exchange Traded Notes (ETN), are similar to ETFs in that they are bought and sold like stocks. The difference is that an ETN is a long-term debt obligation. When you buy an ETN you are loaning your money to a financial institution which in return promises to pay you the equivalent of the return of a given index.

FIXED INCOME INVESTMENTS

In this country we are conditioned to become borrowers. The danger of easy credit is that it has caused us to focus on the loan. Therefore, we've become conditioned to ask questions such as, "which credit card charges us the lowest interest rate (and offers frequent flyer miles)? Where can we obtain the cheapest automobile loan? Where do I get a first mortgage, a second and maybe a third?" All of this in spite of scripture's warning to us:

> *"The rich rules over the poor, and the borrower becomes the lender's slave."*
>
> **— Proverbs 22:7 NAS**

There is another way. Prudent stewards who have money to invest can become lenders instead of borrowers, the head instead of the tail.

Two of the seven asset classes in the Solomon Portfolio, cash and intermediate bonds, are fixed income investments. With a fixed income investment you now become a lender instead of a borrower. Unlike stock ownership you do not own an interest in the company you are lending to. Instead, as a bondholder, you are entitled to regular interest payments from the borrower in addition to the return of your principal when the bond matures. Bondholders may lend to corporations, or governments and municipalities.

Once again, there are literally thousands upon thousands of bond issues to choose from and for the average investor it is nearly impossible to determine which individual bonds to purchase. So, for the Solomon Portfolio we will once again use no-load mutual funds and ETFs to purchase the fixed income portions of the portfolio.

The best and most cost efficient investment vehicles to construct the Solomon Portfolio, are *no-load mutual funds and exchange traded funds and notes.* The next seven chapters will use these tools to discuss and construct each of the seven asset classes necessary to create the Solomon Portfolio.

CHAPTER

4

ASSET CLASS ONE
LARGE CAPITALIZATION
U.S. EQUITIES

"Therefore everyone who hears these words of mine and puts them into practice is like a wise man who built his house on the rock. The rain came down, the streams rose, and the winds blew and beat against that house; yet it did not fall, because it had its foundation on the rock."

—Matthew 7: 24-25

As we now begin to discuss each of the components of the Solomon Portfolio, let's briefly recap what we have already learned.

A. The Solomon Portfolio is comprised of seven core asset classes purchased in equal portions.

B. The seven asset classes are:

1. Large-Cap U.S. stocks

2. Small-Cap U.S. stocks

3. Non-U.S. stocks

4. Intermediate Term U.S. bonds

5. Real Estate Investment Trusts (REITs)

6. Commodities and Natural Resources

7. Cash

C. We will use a combination of highly rated no-load mutual funds and exchange traded funds and notes to construct the Solomon Portfolio. This will keep overall costs down and minimize the amount of individual research you will have to perform while constructing your Solomon Portfolio.

D. Generally, your Solomon Portfolio will be rebalanced once a year.

In this chapter we will discuss **Large Capitalization U.S. Stocks**, also referred to as large-cap stocks. Capitalization is a term that has to do with the outstanding market value of a stock. Large-cap stocks are generally defined as those companies which have over ten billion dollars in investment capitalization (determined by multiplying the number of shares outstanding by the current share price).

Large-cap stocks represent large companies and are generally thought to be more stable than small-cap stocks. Within the large-cap asset class you will find two sub-categories.

The first is **Large-Cap Growth stocks**. Growth stocks are those common stocks that have certain economic attributes (usually a strong history of earnings growth) which lead the prudent investor to believe that this particular stock will outperform other stocks in the same industry. The typical growth stock is a rapidly expanding company which reinvests all of its profits into continued corporate growth. For this reason, growth stocks seldom pay dividends, but often reward their investors with substantial increases in the price of the stock.

The second category of Large-cap U.S. stocks that you need to be familiar with is **Large-Cap U.S. Value Stocks**. Value stocks are those stocks which are believed to be undervalued by prudent investors. An example might be a corporation whose stock price has dropped due to management problems or a poor economy. However, it is believed that the company is now poised to rebound and that the value of the stock will rise at a greater rate than its peers.

There are many, many excellent no-load mutual funds that specialize in just large-cap U.S. growth stocks or large-cap U.S. value stocks. There are also excellent funds that will provide a blend of large-cap growth and value stocks. At the end of this chapter are some funds that have historically performed well in the large-cap U.S. growth, value, or blended market categories.

Another excellent way to determine the "style" of a fund (growth, value or blend) is though the Morningstar style box:

Investment Style Box

Level of risk	Value	Blend	Growth	Market Capitalization
LOW	Large-Cap Value	Large-Cap Blend	Large-Cap Growth	LARGE
MODERATE	Mid-Cap Value	Mid-Cap Blend	Mid-Cap Growth	MEDIUM
HIGH	Small-Cap Value	Small-Cap Blend	Small-Cap Growth	SMALL

The Morningstar style box is a nine-square grid that provides a quick and clear picture of a funds investment style. It is available on each Morningstar report for individual mutual funds. Reprinted with permission of Morningstar, Inc.

By subscribing to Morningstar (**www.morningstar.com** or 312-384-4000) or using one of their online services, it is easy to determine what type of mutual fund you are considering. For instance Morningstar will readily give you the mutual funds investment style, i.e. Large-Cap U.S. Growth Stocks. It will also give you an additional wealth of information regarding a specific fund such as the fund's "star rating", historical results, management fees, contact information and a variety of other very useful information. If you were to use only one research tool in constructing your Solomon Portfolio it should be the services provided by Morningstar. Illustration 4 is a standard Morningstar report on a mutual fund. (Reprinted with permission of Morningstar Inc.)

Large-cap mutual funds should comprise about 14.3% of your Solomon Portfolio. I recommend that you split your investment 50% into large-cap growth funds and 50% into large-cap value funds or that you invest the entire 14.3% into a five star, no-load large-cap blend mutual fund.

Examples of each type of fund follow.

Products mentioned by name in this book (mutual funds, exchange traded funds, exchange traded notes) does not represent an endorsement or guarantee of future performance. Determining investment suitability of individual products, portfolio design, and asset allocation is the sole responsibility of each investor and his/her financial advisor.

LARGE-CAP GROWTH FUNDS	SYMBOL
American Funds Growth Fund	RGAFX
Brandywine Blue	BLUEX
Columbia Marsico 21st Z	NMYAX
Vanguard Growth ETF	VUG

LARGE-CAP VALUE FUNDS	SYMBOL
Columbia Value & Restructuring	UMBIX
Dodge & Cox Stock	DODGX
Excelsior Value & Restructuring	EXBIX
Vanguard Value ETF	VTV

LARGE-CAP BLENDED FUNDS	SYMBOL
CGM Focus	CGMFX
Fairholme	FAIRX
Janus Contrarian	JSVAX
Vanguard TSM ETF	VTI

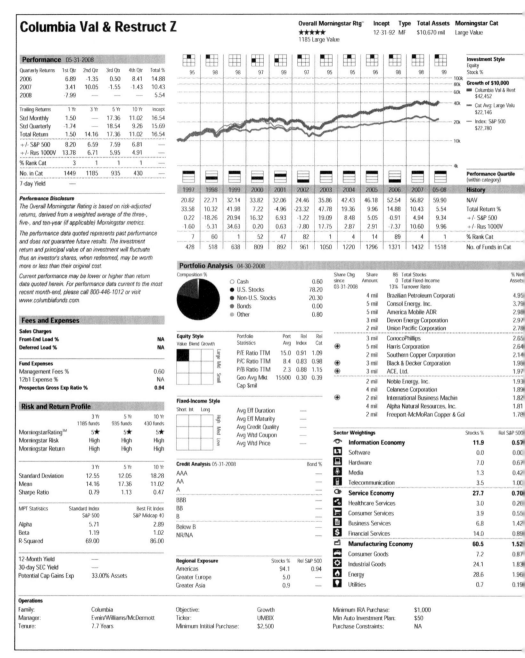

Illustration 4. A standard Morningstar report on a mutual fund. (Reprinted with permission of Morningstar Inc.) Page 1 of 6.

Disclosure for Standardized and Tax Adjusted Returns

The performance data quoted represents past performance and does not guarantee future results. The investment return and principal value of an investment will fluctuate thus an investor's shares, when redeemed, may be worth more or less than their original cost. Current performance may be lower or higher than return data quoted herein. For performance data current to the most recent month-end please visit http://advisor.morningstar.com/familyinfo.asp

An investment in a money market fund is not insured or guaranteed by the FDIC or any other government agency. The current yield quotation more closely reflects the current earnings of the money market fund than the total return quotation. Although money markets seek to preserve the value of your investment at $1.00 per share, it is possible to lose money by investing in the fund.

Standardized Returns assume reinvestment of dividends and capital gains. It depicts performance without adjusting for the effects of taxation, but are adjusted to reflect sales charges and ongoing fund expenses. If adjusted for taxation, the performance quoted would be significantly reduced. For variable annuities, additional expenses will be taken in account, including M&E risk charges, fund-level expenses such as management fees and operating fees, and policy-level administration fees, charges such as surrender, contract and sales charges.

After-tax returns are calculated using the highest individual federal marginal income tax rates, and do not reflect the impact of state and local taxes. Actual after tax returns depend on the investor's tax situation and may differ from those shown. The after tax returns shown are not relevant to investors who hold their fund shares through tax-deferred arrangements such as 401(k) plans or an IRA. After-tax returns exclude the effects of either the alternative minimum tax or phase-out of certain tax credits. Any taxes due are as of the time the distributions are made, and the taxable amount and tax character of each distribution is as specified by the fund on the dividend declaration date. Due to foreign tax credits or realized capital losses, after-tax returns may be greater than before tax returns. After-tax returns for exchange-traded funds are based on net asset value.

Annualized returns 03-31-2008

Standardized Returns (%)	7-day Yield	1Yr	5Yr	10Yr	Since Inception	Inception Date	Max Front Load %	Max Back Load %	Net Exp Ratio %	Gross Exp Ratio %
Columbia Val & Restruct Z	--	-1.74	18.54	9.26	15.69	12-31-92	NA	NA	0.89 ₁	0.94
Standard & Poor's 500	--	-5.08	11.32	3.50	--	--				
Lehman Bro's Agg Bond Index	--	7.67	4.58	6.04	--	--				
MSCI EAFE Index Ndtr_D	--	-2.70	21.40	6.19	--	--				
3 Month T-Bill	--	3.99	3.17	3.63	--	--				

₁ Disclosure: The Advisor has contractually agreed to waive fees and/or reimburse the Fund for certain expenses so that total annual fund operating expenses (exclusive of distribution and servicefees, brokerage commissions, interest, taxes, and extraordinary expenses, but inclusive of custodial charges relating to overdrafts), after giving effect to any balance credits from the Funds custodian, do not exceed 0.98% of the average dailynet assets.

Returns after Taxes (%)	on Distribution					on Distribution and Sales of Shares			
	1Yr	5Yr	10Yr	Since Inception	Inception Date	1Yr	5Yr	10Yr	Since Inception
Columbia Val & Restruct Z	-2.32	18.10	8.90	15.14	12-31-92	-0.92	16.16	8.01	14.16

Illustration 4. A standard Morningstar report on a mutual fund. (Reprinted with permission of Morningstar Inc.) Page 2 of 6.

Mutual Fund Detail Report
Disclosure Statement

The Mutual Fund Detail Report is to be used as supplemental sales literature, and therefore must be preceded or accompanied by the fund's current prospectus and a disclosure statement. Please read the prospectus carefully. In all cases, this disclosure statement should accompany the Mutual Fund Detail Report. Portfolio information is based on the most recent information available to Morningstar.

Morningstar Associates, LLC, a regsitered investment advisor and wholly owned subsidiary of Morningstar, Inc., provides various institutional investment consulting services, including asset allocation advice to investment advisors who have or will be creating a fund-of-fund/asset allocation product. However, despite the fact that such a relationship may exist, the information displayed for those products will not be influenced as they are objective measures and/or derived by quantitative driven formulas (i.e., Morningstar Rating). For more information on these Morningstar relationships, please visit the Release Notes section of this product.

Morningstar is not a FINRA-member firm.

Pre-inception Returns
The analysis in this report may be based, in part, on adjusted historical returns for periods prior to the fund's actual inception. These calculated returns reflect the historical performance of the oldest share class of the fund, adjusted to reflect the fees and expenses of this share class. These fees and expenses are referenced in the report's Performance section.

When pre-inception data are presented in the report, the header at the top of the report will indicate this. In addition, the pre-inception data included in the report will appear in italics.

While the inclusion of pre-inception data provides valuable insight into the probable long-term behavior of newer share classes of a fund, investors should be aware that an adjusted historical return can only provide an approximation of that behavior. For example, the fee structures between a retail share class will vary from that of an institutional share class, as retail shares tend to have higher operating expenses and sales charges. These adjusted historical returns are not actual returns. Calculation methodologies utilized by Morningstar may differ from those applied by other entities, including the fund itself.

Performance
The performance data given represents past perfomance and should not be considered indicative of future results. Principal value and investment return will fluctuate, so that an investor's shares when redeemed may be worth more or less than the original investmant. Fund portfolio statistics change over time. The fund is not FDIC-insured, may lose value and is not guaranteed by a bank or other financial institution.

Total return reflects performance without adjusting for sales charges or the effects of taxation, but is adjusted to reflect all actual ongoing fund expenses and assumes reinvestment of dividends and capital gains. If adjusted for sales charges and the effects of taxation, the performance quoted would be reduced.

Standardized Total Return is reflected as of month- and quarter-end time periods. It depicts performance without adjusting for the effects of taxation, but is adjusted for sales charges, all ongoing fund expenses, and assumes reinvestment of dividends and capital gains. If adjusted for the effects of taxation, the performance quoted would be reduced. The sales charge used in the calculation was obtained from the fund's most recent prospectus and/or shareholder report available to Morningstar. Standardized returns never include pre-inception history.

Morningstar % Rank within Morningstar Category does not account for a fund's sales charge (if applicable). Rankings will not be provided for periods less than one year.

Growth of $10,000
The graph compares the growth of $10,000 in a fund with that of an index and with that of the average for all funds in its Morningstar category. The total returns are not adjusted to reflect sales charges or the effects of taxation, but are adjusted to reflect actual ongoing fund expenses, and assume reinvestment of dividends and capital gains. If adjusted, sales charges would reduce the performance quoted. The index is an unmanaged portfolio of specified securities and cannot be invested in directly. The index and the category average do not reflect any initial or ongoing expenses. A fund's portfolio may differ significantly from the securities in the index. The index is chosen by Morningstar.

If pre-inception data is included in the analysis, it will be graphed.

Risk and Return
The Morningstar Rating is calculated for funds with at least a three-year history. It is calculated based on a Morningstar Risk-Adjusted Return measure that accounts for variation in a fund's monthly performance, placing more emphasis on downward variations and rewarding consistent performance. The top 10% of funds in each category receive 5 stars, the next 22.5% receive 4 stars, the next 35% receive 3 stars, the next 22.5% receive 2 stars and the bottom 10% receive 1 star. The Overall Morningstar Rating for a mutual fund is derived from a weighted average of the performance figures associated with its three-, five- and 10-year (if applicable) Morningstar Rating metrics.

Please note that some Morningstar proprietary calculations, including the Morningstar Rating, may be calculated based on adjusted historical returns (pre-inception returns). If the extended performance rating is in effect, the "stars" are represented as unshaded stars. For each mutual fund with at least a three-year history, Morningstar calculates a Morningstar Rating based on a Morningstar Risk-Adjusted Return measure that accounts for variation in a fund's adjusted monthly performance, placing more emphasis on downward variations and rewarding consistent performance. The top 10% of funds in each category receive 5 stars, the next 22.5% receive 4 stars, the next 35% receive 3 stars, the next 22.5% receive 2 stars and the bottom 10% receive 1 star. This investment's independent Morningstar Rating metric is then compared against the open-end mutual fund universe's actual performance breakpoints to determine its extended performance rating. The Overall Morningstar Rating for a mutual fund is derived from a weighted average of the actual performance figures associated with its three-, five- and 10-year (if applicable) Morningstar Rating metrics.

Morningstar Return rates a mutual fund's performance relative to other funds in its Morningstar Category. It is an assessment of a fund's excess return over a risk-free rate (the return of the 90-day Treasury Bill), after adjusting for all applicable loads and sales charges, in comparison with the mutual funds in its Morningstar Category. In each Morningstar Category, the top 10% of funds earn a High Morningstar Return (HIGH), the next 22.5% Above Average (+AVG), the middle 35% Average (AVG), the next 22.5% Below Averag

Illustration 4. A standard Morningstar report on a mutual fund. (Reprinted with permission of Morningsta Inc.) Page 3 of 6.

(-AVG), and the bottom 10% Low (LOW). Morningstar Return is measured for up to three time periods (three-, five-, and 10 years). These separate measures are then weighted and averaged to produce an overall measure for the mutual fund. Funds with less than three years of performance history are not rated.

Morningstar Risk evaluates a mutual fund's downside volatility relative to that of other funds in its Morningstar Category. It is an assessment of the variations in a fund's monthly returns, with an emphasis on downside variations, in comparison with the mutual funds in its Morningstar Category. In each Morningstar Category, the 10% of funds with the lowest measured risk are described as Low Risk (LOW), the next 22.5% Below Average (-AVG), the middle 35% Average (AVG), the next 22.5% Above Average (+AVG), and the top 10% High (HIGH). Morningstar Risk is measured for up to three time periods (three-, five-, and 10 years). These separate measures are then weighted and averaged to produce an overall measure for the mutual fund. Funds with less than three years of performance history are not rated.

If pre-inception returns are included in this analysis, the risk and return profile data calculated on the basis of these returns will appear in italics.

Risk Measures
The risk measures below are calculated for funds with at least a three-year history.

Standard deviation is a statistical measure of the volatility of the fund's returns.

Mean represents the annualized geometric return for the period shown.

The Sharpe ratio uses standard deviation and excess return to determine reward per unit of risk.

Alpha measures the difference between a fund's actual returns and its expected performance, given its level of risk (as measured by beta). Alpha is often seen as a measure of the value added or subtracted by a portfolio manager.

Beta is a measure of a fund's sensitivity to market movements. A portfolio with a beta greater than 1 is more volatile than the market, and a portfolio with a beta less than 1 is less volatile than the market

R-squared reflects the percentage of a fund's movements that are explained by movements in its benchmark index, showing the degree of correlation between the fund and the benchmark. This figure is also helpful in assessing how likely it is that alpha and beta are statistically significant.

Risk measures calculated using pre-inception data, if included in the analysis, will be presented in italics.

Portfolio Analysis
The Morningstar Style Box reveals a fund's investment strategy. For equity funds the vertical axis shows the market capitalization of the stocks owned and the horizontal axis shows investment style (value, blend or growth). For fixed-income funds the vertical axis shows the average credit quality of the bonds owned, and the horizontal axis shows interest rate sensitivity as measured by a bond's duration (short, intermediate or long).

Equity Portfolio Statistics
The referenced data elements below are a weighted average of the equity holdings in the portfolio.

The Price/Earnings ratio is a weighted average of the price/earnings ratios of the stocks in the underlying fund's portfolio. The P/E ratio of a stock is calculated by dividing the current price of the stock by its trailing 12-months' earnings per share. In computing the average, Morningstar weights each portfolio holding by the percentage of equity assets it represents.

The Price/Cash Flow ratio is a weighted average of the price/cash-flow ratios of the stocks in a fund's portfolio. Price/cash-flow shows the ability of a business to generate cash and acts as a gauge of liquidity and solvency.

The Price/Book ratio is a weighted average of the price/book ratios of all the stocks in the underlying fund's portfolio. The P/B ratio of a company is calculated by dividing the market price of its stock by the company's per-share book value. Stocks with negative book values are excluded from this calculation.

The geometric average market capitalization of a fund's equity portfolio offers a measure of the size of the companies in which the mutual fund invests.

Fixed-Income Portfolio Statistics
The referenced data elements below are a weighted average of the fixed income holdings in the portfolio.

Duration is a time measure of a bond's interest rate sensitivity. Average effective duration is a weighted average of the duration of the underlying fixed income securities within the portfolio.

Average effective maturity is a weighted average of all the maturities of the bonds in a portfolio, computed by weighting each maturity date by the market value of the security.

Average credit quality is calculated by taking the weighted average of the credit rating for each bond in the portfolio.

Average weighted coupon is generated from the fund's portfolio by weighting the coupon of each bond by its relative size in the portfolio. Coupons are fixed percentages paid out on a fixed-income security on an annual basis.

Average weighted price is generated from the fund's portfolio by weighting the price of each bond by its relative size in the portfolio. This number reveals if the fund favors bonds selling at prices above or below face value (premium or discount securities, respectively). A higher number indicates a bias toward premiums. This statistic is expressed as a percentage of par (face) value.

Turnover Ratio is a decent proxy for how frequently a manager trades his or her portfolio. The inverse of a fund's turnover ratio is the average holding period for a security in the fund. As turnover increases, a fund's brokerage costs typically rise as well.

Operations
Purchase constraints denote if a mutual fund has any of the following qualities: Qualified Access (A), Institutional (T), Closed to New Investments, (C) or Closed to All Investments (L). Because these qualities can all act as restrictions and/or requirements for investment, they are grouped together.

Potential capital gains exposure is the percentage of a mutual fund's total assets that represent capital appreciation.

Illustration 4. A standard Morningstar report on a mutual fund. (Reprinted with permission of Morningstar Inc.) Page 4 of 6.

Investment Risk

International Funds/Emerging Market Funds: The investor should note that funds that invest in international securities involve special additional risks. These risks include, but are not limited to, currency risk, political risk, and risk associated with varying accounting standards. Investing in emerging markets may accentuate these risks.

Sector Funds: The investor should note that funds that invest exclusively in one sector or industry involve additional risks. The lack of industry diversification subjects the investor to increased industry-specific risks.

Non-Diversified Funds: The investor should note that funds that invest more of their assets in a single issuer involve additional risks, including share price fluctuations, because of the increased concentration of investments.

Small-Cap Funds: The investor should note that funds that invest in stocks of small companies involve additional risks. Smaller companies typically have a higher risk of failure, and are not as well established as larger blue-chip companies. Historically, smaller-company stocks have experienced a greater degree of market volatility that the overall market average.

Mid Cap Funds: The investor should note that funds that invest in companies with market capitalization below $10 billion involve additional risks. The securities of these companies may be more volatile and less liquid than the securities of larger companies.

High-Yield Bond Funds: The investor should note that funds that invest in lower-rated debt securities (commonly referred as junk bonds) involve additional risks because of the lower credit quality of the securities in the portfolio. The investor should be aware of the possible higher level of volatility, and increased risk of default.

Tax-Free Municipal Bond Funds: The investor should note that the income from tax-free municipal bond funds may be subject to state and local taxation and the Alternative Minimum Tax.

Illustration 4. A standard Morningstar report on a mutual fund. (Reprinted with permission of Morningstar Inc.) Page 5 of 6.

Benchmark Disclosure

Russell 1000 Value TR
Tracks the companies within the Russell 1000 with lower price-to-book
ratios and lower forecasted growth values.

S&P 500 TR
A market capitalization-weighted index of 500 widely held stocks often
used as a proxy for the stock market.

S&P Midcap 400 TR
This index is comprised of stocks in the middle-capitalization range,
and includes approximately 10% of the capitalization of U.S. equity securities.

Illustration 4. A standard Morningstar report on a mutual fund. (Reprinted with permission of Morningstar Inc.) Page 6 of 6.

CHAPTER

5

ASSET CLASS TWO
SMALL CAPITALIZATION U.S. STOCKS

"Listen! A farmer went out to sow his seed. As he was scattering the seed, some fell along the path, and the birds came and ate it up. Some fell on rocky places, where it did not have much soil. It sprang up quickly, because the soil was shallow. But when the sun came up, the plants were scorched, and they withered because they had no root. Other seed fell among thorns, which grew up and choked the plants, so that they did not bear grain. Still other seed fell on good soil. It came up, grew and produced a crop, multiplying thirty, sixty, or even a hundred times."

—Mark 4:3-8

Although this parable is expressly about the planting of God's Word into the hearts of men, it is an appropriate analogy for the planting of small businesses as well. Every year thousands of small businesses are planted in this country. While most fail for a variety of reasons, several small businesses become major successes. In constructing the Solomon Portfolio we are looking for a way to invest in those successful small businesses that will provide a return of thirty, sixty or even hundred times on our investment.

The second asset class in the Solomon Portfolio is **Small-cap U.S. stocks.**

Small businesses are the backbone of the American economy. About one-half of all U.S. workers are employed by small businesses. A small business is defined as a company with less than five-hundred employees. It is not an exaggeration to say that this great country has been built by men and women with great ideas who had the freedom to bring those ideas to the market place in the form of small businesses. Every Solomon Portfolio must contain a share of small-cap U.S. stocks representing the great new business ideas of the present and the future.

As you look at the Morningstar style box you can see that small-cap U.S. stocks represent smaller companies having a higher investment risk associated with them. Small-cap U.S. stocks will generally have a market capitalization of two-billion dollars or less. Remember that market capitalization is only an indication of a corporation's size (number of shares outstanding times the current price). Many small-cap U.S. stocks are extremely successful companies that often become large-cap U.S. stocks over time.

Small-cap U.S. stocks carry a high standard deviation for risk and are therefore more volatile than their large-cap counterparts. For instance, a small-cap growth fund will have more dramatic ups and downs than a large-cap growth fund, but they will also have a higher potential for return. Over the last thirty-eight years the standard deviation of return for large-cap U.S. stocks, small-cap U.S. stocks and non-U.S. equities have been 16.61, 21.69 and 21.54 respectively (the higher the standard deviation, the higher the risk). However, the average annual return for those three asset classes during the same time period has been 11.03% for large-cap U.S. stocks, 11.74% for small-cap U.S. stocks, and 10.86% for non-U.S. stocks.

One possible drawback with smaller companies is that they may be driven by a single product. So the success or failure of that product can either catapult the price of its stock to lofty levels or bring it crashing down. This is all the more reason why you should invest in high quality no-load small-cap mutual funds and exchange traded funds which allow you to diversify your holdings within an asset class.

When investing in small-cap U.S. stocks you will also want to diversify into growth and value stocks as we discussed in the last chapter. Examples of each type of fund follow:

Products mentioned by name in this book (mutual funds, exchange traded funds, exchange traded notes) does not represent an endorsement or guarantee of future performance. Determining investment suitability of individual products, portfolio design, and asset allocation is the sole responsibility of each investor and his/her financial advisor.

SMALL-CAP GROWTH FUNDS	SYMBOL
Janus Triton	JATTX
UMB Scout Small Cap	UMBHX
iShares S&P 600 Growth ETF	IJT

SMALL-CAP VALUE FUNDS	SYMBOL
Bridgeway Small Cap Value	BRSVX
Columbia Small Cap Value	NSVAX
Vanguard Small Cap Value ETF	VBR

SMALL-CAP BLENDED FUNDS	SYMBOL
Royce Value Inv	RVVHX
Vanguard Tax-Managed Small Cap	VTMSX
iShares S&P 600 Sm Cap 600 ETF	IJR

CHAPTER

6

ASSET CLASS THREE
NON-U.S. STOCKS

"For the King (Solomon) had a fleet of ships of Tarshish at sea with the fleet of Hiram. Once every three years the fleet of Tarshish came bringing gold, silver, ivory, apes and peacocks."

—1 Kings 10:22 (Amplified, parenthesis added)

If King Solomon had international interests, then it is certainly something we too should consider as one of the asset classes within the Solomon Portfolio. This third asset class we are going to include in our portfolio is **non-U.S. stocks**.

There are several types of non-U.S. stock funds from which to choose and several terms that you will need to be familiar with in order to construct this portion of your portfolio.

International funds: a basic international fund will diversify across a broad spectrum of countries and companies all of which will be non-U.S. companies. These funds usually fall into one of two sub-categories. The more conservative international funds will invest in *established countries and companies*. Typically these countries can be found in Europe, Australia and the Far East. The performance of these funds is usually tracked against a benchmark called the *MS EAFE* or Morgan Stanley Europe, Australasia and Far East Index.

Another sub-category is known as *Emerging Market Funds*. As the name implies, these funds invest in smaller countries with economies that are beginning to flourish in response to the spread of capitalism and the creation of their own stock markets. Examples might be Turkey, Mexico, Malaysia, Chili, Taiwan, Jordan, Thailand and many more. The prices of these funds can be very volatile as they are subject to political risks, currency speculation, and poorly capitalized companies with questionable accounting standards. Morgan Stanley also has a benchmark for emerging markets called the *MS EMF* or Morgan Stanley Emerging Markets Free Index. This index tracks stock markets in seven emerging markets selected because of their openness to foreign investors.

Emerging Market funds are not for the faint hearted. Although emerging markets have produced excellent returns in some years, it has certainly been a wild ride in terms of price swings. As you construct the Non-U.S. Stock portion of your Solomon Portfolio, you want to minimize your emerging market exposure to 10%–15% of your total non-U.S. Stock holdings.

Global Mutual Funds: invest in stocks throughout the world including American stocks (whereas **international funds** are restricted to investing in foreign markets only). The reasoning here is that because many U.S. companies are really international companies in scope, they should be included in global funds.

There are some foreign funds that are very narrow in scope, investing in only one country, such as Viet Nam or China. My advice to you would be to avoid funds that are this narrowly focused, in favor of a combination of high quality international and global funds that include some emerging market exposure.

Examples of each type of fund follow.

Products mentioned by name in this book (mutual funds, exchange traded funds, exchange traded notes) does not represent an endorsement or guarantee of future performance. Determining investment suitability of individual products, portfolio design, and asset allocation is the sole responsibility of each investor and his/her financial advisor.

INTERNATIONAL, GLOBAL, AND EMERGING MARKET FUNDS	SYMBOL
Columbia Marsico Intl	NMOAX
Dodge & Cox Intl Stock	DODFX
Harbor Intl Instl	HAINX
Manning & Napier World Opportunity	EXWAX
Masters' Select International Equity	MSILX
UMB Scout International	UMBWX
iShares S&P Glb Cons Stpls ETF	KXI
Vanguard EmergMkts ETF	VWO
Vanguard FTSE AW ETF	VEU

CHAPTER

7

ASSET CLASS FOUR
COMMODITIES
AND NATURAL RESOURCES

"Solomon's daily provisions were thirty cors of fine flour and sixty cors of meal, ten head of stall-fed cattle, twenty of pasture-fed cattle and a hundred sheep and goats, as well as deer, gazelles, roebucks and choice fowl. Solomon had four thousand stalls for chariot horses and twelve thousand horses. The district officers, each in his month, supplied provisions for King Solomon and all who came to the king's table. They saw to it that nothing was lacking. They brought to the proper place their quotas of barley and straw for the chariot horses and the other horses."

—1 Kings 4:22-23, 26-28

The fourth asset class in the Solomon Portfolio is **commodities** and **natural resources**. Commodities and natural resources are bulk goods such as, oil, natural gas, industrial metals, precious metals, all grains, cattle, sugar, cotton, coffee, etc. It is extremely risky, even impossible for the average investor to go out into the various commodity markets and try to purchase the various commodities and natural resources needed to provide a balanced commodity and natural resource component for the Solomon Portfolio.

Fortunately, there are a variety of no-load mutual funds and exchange traded funds and exchange traded notes that will allow you to purchase a representative "basket of commodities and natural resources" by purchasing the no-load mutual fund or ETF or ETN.

I want to stress again, when adding the Commodity and Natural Resource Asset Class to your portfolio, you should not go out and purchase individual commodities or any type of commodity futures contract. This is an exceptionally risky business that should be left to professional commodity traders. The Solomon Portfolio attains its commodity component solely through no-load mutual funds and ETFs and ETNs.

As you begin your research, you will want to know the allocation of commodities within a particular fund or ETF/ETN. For instance, no-load natural resource mutual funds tend to be more heavily weighted in oil and gas holdings. Whereas, ETFs and ETNs will provide a much broader portfolio of all commodities.

There are also benchmarks that you can compare your commodity fund to. Two well known benchmarks are **Dow Jones-AIG Commodity Index (DJ-AIGCI)** which is a rolling index of 20 physical commodities. Another well known index is the **Standard & Poor's Goldman Sachs Commodity Index (S&P-GSCI)** which is a very sophisticated weighted index of 26 commodities from all commodity sectors.

ETFs and ETNs will often be created to try and reflect the results of one of these indexes. For instance, the ETN symbol **DJP** has the stated purpose of trying to represent the Dow Jones-AIG Commodity Index Total Return.

Examples of commodity investments follow:

Products mentioned by name in this book (mutual funds, exchange traded funds, exchange traded notes) does not represent an endorsement or guarantee of future performance. Determining investment suitability of individual products, portfolio design and asset allocation is the sole responsibility of each investor and his/her financial advisor.

COMMODITY ETFs AND ETNs	SYMBOL
iPath Dow Jones-AIG Agriculture Total Return Sub-Index	JJA
iPath Dow Jones-AIG Commodity Index total Return	DJP
iShares S&P GSCI Commodity Index Trust	GSG
iPath S&P GSCI Total Return Index	GSP
RICI-Total Return Elements	RJI
Rogers International Commodity Index-Agriculture	RJA

NATURAL RESOURCE NO-LOAD MUTUAL FUNDS	SYMBOL
Ivy Global Natural Resources	IGNIX
T. Rowe Price New Era	PRNEX
US Global Inv Global Resources	PSPFX

CHAPTER

8

ASSET CLASS FIVE
REAL ESTATE

"And Solomon ruled over all the kingdoms from the River to the land of the Philistines, as far as the border of Egypt. These countries brought tribute and were Solomon's subjects all his life."

—1 Kings 4:21

The fifth asset class in the Solomon Portfolio is **real estate**.

Just as we did not acquire commodities and natural resources by buying the actual commodity, we are not going to acquire the real estate asset class by going out and purchasing a variety of apartment buildings, shopping centers, hospitals and other commercial and residential type properties. Once again, we will be using real estate no-load mutual funds, and exchange traded funds and notes to attain the real estate asset class portion of the Solomon Portfolio.

These funds will generally invest in real estate investment trusts (REITs). A REIT is a company that manages a portfolio of real estate for a profit. A REIT can contain virtually any type of real estate investment including, apartment buildings, shopping centers, warehouses, hotels, hospitals, office buildings, etc. REITs typically have excellent yields as they are required by law to distribute 95% of their net earnings to shareholders each year in order to maintain favorable REIT income tax status with the IRS. This cash distribution generally provides a steady stream of income to shareholders which can smooth out some of the volatility of the fluctuating values of the underlying real estate investments in a REIT.

Like commodity funds, real estate funds are diversifiers. That is, they generally have a very low correlation to stocks. So when the stock market goes down, real estate funds will tend to move in the opposite direction. Equally important is the fact that real estate has a negative correlation to the bond market. When interest rates are low it pushes up the price of housing and other real estate investments and when interest rates are high it often forces the value of real estate down. Since real estate funds will tend to move in the opposite direction of both stocks and bonds they are excellent for stabilizing a portfolio and moving its overall correlation towards zero.

Examples of Real Estate investments follow:

Products mentioned by name in this book (mutual funds, exchange traded funds, exchange traded notes) does not represent an endorsement or guarantee of future performance. Determining investment suitability of individual products, portfolio design, and asset allocation is the sole responsibility of each investor and his/her financial advisor.

REAL ESTATE INVESTMENT MUTUAL FUNDS	SYMBOL
Alpine Intl Real Estate	EGLRX
CGM Realty	CGMRX
JennDry Dry Gbl Real Estate	PURZX
Third Avenue Real Estate Value	TAREX
iShares C&S Realty ETF	ICF
Vanguard REIT Index ETF	VNQ

CHAPTER

9

ASSET CLASS SIX

CASH

"And now let Pharaoh appoint commissioners over the land to take a fifth of the harvest of Egypt during the seven years of abundance. They should collect all the food of these good years that are coming and store up the grain under the authority of Pharaoh, to be kept in the cities for food. This food should be held in reserve for the country, to be used during the seven years of famine that will come upon Egypt, so that the country may not be ruined by the famine."

—Genesis 41:33-36

We cannot make it out of the first book of the Bible without the Lord teaching us the importance of preparing for emergencies. The story of Joseph shows us, among other things, how the Lord used one man to save a nation by storing up the basics for the inevitable hard times that were to come.

The sixth asset class in the Solomon Portfolio is a **cash reserve.** Life happens.

"In this world you will have trouble."

—John 16:33

It is not a question of if; it is a question of when. People lose jobs, children get sick, cars break down, and unexpected expenses, like unwelcome guests, come knocking at your door. One of the foundational elements of good financial stewardship is establishing a fund for emergencies. This Biblical principle of establishing a reserve for emergencies is still as valid for us today as it was in the days of Joseph as he counseled with the Pharaoh. However, it is often not practical for us to store food; therefore our reserve is readily available cash.

The question then is how we invest that cash in order to receive some return on our investment while still maintaining it as the safest and most readily available component of our Solomon Portfolio.

There are three basic investments that I would consider suitable for this investment class:

1. Money Market Accounts
2. Money Market Funds
3. Certificates of Deposit

Let's discuss each of these in terms of their safety, liquidity and yield.

MONEY MARKET ACCOUNTS

Money market accounts are generally offered by banks and credit unions.

Developed in the early 1980s they are a cross between a higher interest paying savings account and a checking account. They offer a non-fluctuating $1 investment value (your principal is never at risk) and a competitive interest rate for this asset class.

> **SAFETY** — Money market accounts are insured up to $100,000 by federal agencies. Do not confuse money market *accounts* with money market *funds* which are not federally insured.

> **LIQUIDITY** — Generally, there are two ways to gain immediate access to the cash in your money market account. You can write a limited number of checks on the account (usually three per month) or you can transfer cash from your money market account into one of your other accounts within the same financial institution.

> **YIELD** — Money market account interest rates are allowed to "float," therefore, they stay competitive with similar investments at other financial institutions. Your deposits are credited with interest on a daily basis. Most money market accounts require a minimum balance to open the account.

MONEY MARKET FUNDS

A money market fund is legally a mutual fund that is generally offered by stockbrokerage firms and mutual fund companies. The funds pool the cash of millions of investors and lend it to large corporations, banks and governments on a short-term basis. The earnings on these loans, less the money market fund's management fee, are then credited to your account in the form of a dividend.

Theoretically, a money market fund is also based on a non-fluctuating $1 value, however, they are mutual funds, not bank accounts, and there is the remote chance that you could lose some of your original investment if the "dollar is broken". This has never happened in the history of the money market fund industry and the general consensus among investment advisors is that the money market funds of sound established firms are a safe investment.

SAFETY — Due to the short-term nature of a money market fund's investments and the relatively conservative nature of what they invest in, almost everyone agrees that money market funds are a very safe investment.

LIQUIDITY — Almost all money market funds offer 24-hour redemption by phone, wire transfer, or check.

YIELD — Money market funds are very competitive and offer excellent short-term interest rates. Since they are not federally insured like money market accounts, their interest rates are generally marginally higher.

CERTIFICATES OF DEPOSIT

A certificate of deposit is a debt instrument issued by a bank whereby you agree to loan them your funds for a specified period of time (weeks to years) and they agree to pay you interest in return (based on the current marketplace). You should only purchase certificates of deposit from banks that offer FDIC insurance. This insurance will cover your losses up to $100,000.

SAFETY – Certificates of Deposit are insured up to $100,000 by the FDIC or the NCUA and, therefore, are very safe.

LIQUIDITY – Banking institutions can issue CDs with maturities ranging from 7 days up to several years. Usually the longer the investment term of the certificate, the higher the interest rate you can earn. It is important to note that if you need your money prior to the maturity date of the certificate of deposit; a penalty will be imposed for the premature withdrawal of your funds. Since we are using these CDs as the "cash" portion of your Solomon Portfolio for this reason you should keep your maturity dates under one year.

YIELD – The interest rate paid on CDs is unregulated and can vary substantially. Aggressive banks trying to attract new deposits will often offer higher than average interest rates to entice you to open an account with them.

Many major brokerage firms such as Charles Schwab & Co., Inc. will make available CDs from bank offerings all across the country. By going to their website you will be able to see a matrix of offerings based on maturity dates and yields. This is often a good way to purchase CDs as the rates are competitive, the CDs you purchase all show up on one monthly statement and they still maintain their FDIC insurance.

Examples of Money Market Funds and CD sources follow:

Products mentioned by name in this book (mutual funds, exchange traded funds, exchange traded notes) does not represent an endorsement or guarantee of future performance. Determining investment suitability of individual products, portfolio design, and asset allocation is the sole responsibility of each investor and his/her financial advisor.

TAXABLE MONEY MARKEY FUNDS	SYMBOL
Schwab Value Advantage	SWVXX
T. Rowe Price Prime Reserve	PRRXX
Vanguard Prime Money Market	VMMXX

U.S. TREASURY MONEY MARKET FUNDS	SYMBOL
Vanguard Admiral Treasury Money Market	VUSXX
Vanguard Treasury Money Market	VMPXX

MUNICIPAL TAX-FREE MONEY MARKET FUNDS	SYMBOL
T. Rowe Price Summit Municipal Money Market	TRSXX
Vanguard Tax-Exempt Money Market	VMSXX

SOURCES OF CDs

www.schwab.com

CHAPTER

10

ASSET CLASS SEVEN
INTERMEDIATE BONDS

"For the Lord your God will bless you as He has promised, and you will lend to many nations but will borrow from none."

—Deuteronomy 15:6

Record deficits, record consumer debt, the largest debtor nation in the world.... We have forgotten that:

"The rich rules over the poor, And the borrower becomes the lender's slave."

—Proverbs 22:7 (New American Standard)

Most of us do not consider that there is another way. Wise stewards who have money to invest can become lenders instead of borrowers...the head instead of the tail.

One of the most efficient and secure methods of becoming a lender is by investing in the seventh asset class of the Solomon Portfolio, intermediate bonds. Bonds are promissory notes between a lender (in this case you) and a borrower (referred to as the issuer) usually a corporation, government or a governmental agency. The bond will explain when the issuer will repay the original principal borrowed from the lender. It also explains, in detail, when and how much interest will be paid to the lender until the loan is repaid in full.

Once again, I do not recommend that you go out and buy individual bonds from a broker. Rather, you should purchase high quality, no-load, short-term and intermediate term bond mutual funds. Make no mistake, you will still have to do your homework as there are many types of intermediate bond funds. It will take time and understanding to determine which type fund is best for you.

There are many concepts that you need to be familiar with when purchasing bonds funds.

MATURITY: refers to that point in time when the bond pays you back the money you originally lent to the borrower. When comparing bond funds you will want to determine what the average maturity is of the bonds that the funds hold. This information is readily available in the fund prospectus or through Morningstar. The average maturity for intermediate bond funds should be between five and ten years.

INTEREST RATE SENSITIVITY: this concept refers to the fact that interest rates and bond prices move in opposite directions. When interest rates rise, the value of your underlying bonds decline. If you sell it at this point you will not get back your original investment. Your only alternative is to wait for the bond to mature. At maturity a bond will pay back it original face value. ***DURATION*** is a means of measuring this interest rate risk. Duration tells you the sensitivity of bond funds to changes in interest rates. For instance, a bond fund with duration of ten years means that if interest rates rise by 1%, then the value of the bond fund will drop by 10%. You should search the bond fund prospectus to find out the duration of the particular fund you are interested in purchasing.

SAFETY: Bonds are only as safe as the entity which issues them is financially secure. Some bonds offer specific collateral as security; others rely on the strength of the issuer to imply safety, such as government bonds, for example. Bonds are rated for safety by two major credit rating companies: Moody's and Standard & Poors. These ratings are:

	Moody's	Standard & Poors
Prime	Aaa	AAA
Excellent	Aa	AA
Good	A	A
Average	Baa	BBB
Fair	Ba	BB
Poor	B	—
Marginal	Caa	B
Default	Ca	D

A bond fund prospectus or Morningstar report will tell you what percentage of each type of bond a fund holds in its portfolio. Generally, the higher percentage of highly rated bonds in a portfolio, the lower the yield will be and vice versa.

TYPES: Intermediate bond funds will come in many types including:

1. Corporate bond funds issued by companies which pay interest, which is taxable.

2. Municipal bond funds which are issued by state and local governments. The interest paid is federal income tax free, and if you live in the state of the issuer you pay no state income tax as well. These bonds are excellent for individuals in high tax brackets.

3. Treasury bond funds hold bonds issued by the US government. They are state income tax exempt, but are taxable for federal income tax purposes. Generally these are considered the safest of all bond funds in their class and therefore usually pay the lowest interest rates.

4. International bonds are issued by foreign issuers. These bonds are much riskier due to currency fluctuations, foreign taxes that may be applied to the interest paid, as well as the potential for political unrest.

5. Mortgage backed funds specialize in buying mortgages and collecting the interest payments. The repayment of the principal on these bonds is usually guaranteed at the bonds maturity by government sanctioned entities such as GNMA or FNMA.

FEES: when selecting a no-load bond fund, be very careful to understand the fees charged by the mutual fund company itself. Any fee over 1/2% per year is excessive, as it will eat up too much of interest income paid to you by the fund.

Examples of Intermediate Bond Fund investments follow:

Products mentioned by name in this book (mutual funds, exchange traded funds, exchange traded notes) does not represent an endorsement or guarantee of future performance. Determining investment suitability of individual products, portfolio design, and asset allocation is the sole responsibility of each investor and his/her financial advisor.

INTERMEDIATE BOND MUTUAL FUNDS	SYMBOL
Dodge & Cox Income	DODIX
Harbor Bond Fund	HABDX
Managers Fremont Bond	MBDFX
TCW Total Return	TGLMX
Vanguard GNMA	VFIIX
Vanguard Inflation Prot Securities	VIPSX
iShares Lehman TIPS Bonds ETF	TIP

CHAPTER

11

THE SOLOMON PORTFOLIO

"Give portions to seven..."

—Ecclesiastes 11:2

Now that we have discussed each of the seven core asset classes of the Solomon Portfolio it is time to construct a sample portfolio of $100,000.

Products mentioned by name in this book (mutual funds, exchange traded funds, exchange traded notes) does not represent an endorsement or guarantee of future performance. Determining investment suitability of individual products, portfolio design, and asset allocation is the sole responsibility of each investor and his/her financial advisor.

THE SOLOMON PORTFOLIO: $100,000 PORTFOLIO ILLUSTRATION

CATEGORY AND FUND	SYMBOL	$ INVESTED
1. LARGE-CAP U.S. FUNDS:		
LARGE-CAP U.S. GROWTH		
BRANDYWINE BLUE	BLUEX	$7,150
LARGE-CAP U.S. VALUE		
EXCELSIOR VAL & RESTR	UMBIX	7,150
2. SMALL-CAP U.S. FUNDS:		
SMALL-CAP U.S. GROWTH		
JANUS TRITON	JATTX	7,150
SMALL-CAP U.S. VALUE		
BRIDGEWAY SM-CAP	BRSVX	7,150
3. INTERNATIONAL STOCKS:		
UMB SCOUT INTL	UMBWX	14,300
4. COMMODITIES & NATURAL RES:		
iPATH DJ-AIGCom	DJP	7,150
US GLOBAL INV RES	PSPFX	7,150
5. REAL ESTATE:		
ALPINE INTL REAL EST	EGLRX	7,150
CGM REALTY	CGMRX	7,150
6. INTERMEDIATE BONDS:		
MANAGERS FREMONT BD	MBDFX	7,150
VANGUARD INFLATION PROT	VIPSX	7,150
7. CASH:		
VANGUARD PRIME MMKT	VMMXX	14,200
TOTAL SOLOMON PORTFOLIO INITIAL VALUE		**$100,000**

"Solomon's wisdom was greater than the wisdom of all the men of the East, and greater than all the wisdom of Egypt. He was wiser than any other man,.......Men of all nations came to listen to Solomon's wisdom, sent by all the kings of the world, who had heard of his wisdom."

—1 Kings 4:30-31, 34

Now you know too.

The wisdom that the Lord gave to Solomon over 3,000 years ago has been passed down to you as well. No longer does investing have to be a mystery. If you will follow the simple instructions in this book, investing your funds will become easy and profitable.

Why so easy, why so profitable? Because you are walking in the wisdom of King Solomon under the guidance of the Lord who created you, loves you, and wants you to prosper.

"Beloved, I pray that in all respects you may prosper and be in good health, just as your soul prospers."

—3 John 2, New American Standard

CHAPTER

12

THE EIGHTH PORTION
THE READER'S GIFT

"Give portions to seven, yes to eight, for you do not know what disaster may come upon the land."

—Ecclesiastes 11:2

I have to admit to you that for years I knew that Ecclesiastes 11:2 held the key to the Lord's plan for asset allocation. However, I would still ask the Lord to clarify this verse for me, "Which is it? Are we to allocate our assets into seven portions or eight?" The answer I heard was, "Yes".

But, I know that every word of scripture is true and with purpose.

"All scripture is God breathed and is useful for teaching, rebuking, correcting and training in righteousness, so that the man of God may be thoroughly equipped for every good work."

—2 Timothy 3:16-17

And,

"God is not a God of disorder but of peace (and order)"

—1 Corinthians 14:33 (insert from Amplified version).

What these two scriptures tell us is that every word in the Bible was placed there by God and it has a distinct and purposeful reason for being there. It was my job to find out why it says "seven, yes eight" and the only way to do that was through prayer.

After much prayer and study the Lord showed me that the **Solomon Portfolio** is the asset allocation model that is suitable and profitable for the vast majority of investors.

For the majority of people reading this book the seven asset class Solomon Portfolio is the only investment strategy you will ever need.

However, the Lord explained to me that some people have been given special gifts and talents in investing, and for them, an eighth portion is permissible.

For instance, some people have a great talent for developing real estate projects. For them, in addition to general real estate investments, they may have specific real estate projects that they develop and own as an eighth portion. Another excellent example would be in the area of collectibles. Collectibles such as art, coins, stamps, antiques, old books, manuscripts or maps, vintage automobiles, baseball cards, etc. may all qualify as an eight portion due to a special talent a person may have.

A word of caution, not all collectibles are a "portion" meant as an investment portion. Most collections are just for fun, a hobby, and it is important that a potential collector knows the difference. Not all investors, (in my opinion very few), should have an eighth portion. I say this because the eighth portion is usually not very liquid or easy to understand. It is slow to appreciate in value, it requires highly specialized knowledge, and it is usually subject to volatile increases and decreases in value. For this reason, if you intend to pursue an eighth portion as an investment option, it is important that you understand the following basic rules:

1. **First, you must have the love.** The eighth portion should spring from a God given passion within you for whatever that portion is. Be it real estate development or collecting art, you must have a passion for the portion.

2. **Gain knowledge.** The eighth portion often requires highly specialized knowledge and/or advanced education that is gained over a long period of time. Developing a real estate project is highly complex work. Collectibles are perhaps the most difficult group of assets to value and without a sound understanding of the collectible and the market for that collectible, it is easy to overpay for your purchase. For example, stocks are traded over huge national exchanges; therefore you know the current value of a stock at the exact same time as any other potential buyer. However, if you walk into an antique store armed with a checkbook and very little knowledge, chances

are you will pay dearly for your first lesson on the fair market value of a Chippendale chair.

3. **Be patient.** Real estate projects appreciate slowly and require much work along the way. Collections are a labor of love and they tend to increase in value slowly as well. This is why you should collect only what you have a passion for and only after your financial house (the seven core asset classes) is in order.

4. **Protect your investment.** Real estate will require many forms of insurance to protect it while you own it. Collections often need special care and attention. Make sure that you do everything necessary to protect your collection from the ravages of time and store them in a safe and secure place.

Of course real estate projects and collectibles are only examples of what an eighth portion may be. The Lord may have given you other gifts and talents that will qualify as an eighth investment portion. However, I want to stress once again that it is my experience that by far **the majority of people are best served by sticking to the seven asset class model described in this book.**

EPILOGUE
DO YOU KNOW JESUS?

The purpose of my books is not to make you rich; it is always to make you a better steward of what the Lord has entrusted into your care. Scripture tells us that if you are faithful with the little than He can trust you with more. Please remember that no matter how wealthy you become, it is all fleeting. We are blessed to be a blessing. Someday we will all stand before God and he will ask us two questions.

1. What did you do with my son Jesus Christ? And,

2. What did you do with the people that I put into your life?

How we are able to answer the first question will determine where we spend eternity. How we answer the second question will determine our eternal rewards or lack thereof. It is that simple.

So, therefore, my heartfelt desire is that this book has moved you toward a closer relationship with the Lord. If you do not know Jesus Christ as your personal Lord and Savior now is the time, He is calling your name. You can respond by saying the following prayer:

Lord Jesus, I am a sinner in need of a Savior. I believe that you are the Son of God and that you died on the cross, a living sacrifice for my sins. I surrender my life to You. Please forgive me for my sins and create in me a new heart that desires to serve You all the days of my life. I accept You as my Lord and Savior. Amen

If you have prayed this prayer I urge you to do three things:

1. Get a good easy to read Bible and begin to read it everyday, start with the gospel of Matthew.

2. Find a good church that teaches the Bible as the perfect word of God.

3. Begin to pray everyday, just have a simple conversation with your Creator; I know He is waiting to hear from you.

ABOUT THE AUTHOR

ROBERT W. KATZ, CPA/PFS, MS, has been a partner in a New Orleans-based certified public accounting firm for the last 30 years. His areas of specialty include personal financial planning, tax and estate planning and investment consulting. He received his bachelor's degree from Louisiana State University and a master's degree from the University of New Orleans. He is a Certified Public Accountant, AICPA Personal Financial Specialist, and an ordained minister. Bob is the author of several Christian financial planning books and articles including *Money Came by the House the Other Day*, *Money Came by the House the Other Day Study Guide* and *Biblical Roads to Financial Freedom*. He has been a frequent guest on Christian television shows such as *Enjoying Everyday Life* with Joyce Meyer, *The 700 Club* with Pat Robertson, *This is Your Day!* with Benny Hinn, and *Life Today* with James Robison.

He resides in Mandeville, Louisiana with his wife, Jamie and their two children.

You can contact **Robert Katz** at:

Email: rwkatz@katzgallagher.com

OTHER BOOKS BY ROBERT KATZ:
Money Came by the House the Other Day
Money Came by the House the Other Day Study Guide
Biblical Roads to Financial Freedom

You can purchase all of Robert Katz's books and tapes at his website:

www.robertkatzministries.com

You can contact **Professor Craig L. Israelsen** at:

Craig@TDBench.com

Or visit his website at:

www.TBench.com